W9-ADL-321

RECEIVED
OCT 29 2015
By_____

SAMMY SPIDER'S

FIRST

TASTE OF HANUKKAH
A Cookbook

Sylvia A. Rouss and Genene Levy Turndorf

Illustrated by
Katherine Janus Kahn

KAR-BEN
PUBLISHING

To my grandchildren, Hayden, Derek, Leo and Eden who are always the sweetest delights in my kitchen. —S.A.R.

To my children, Max and Lily, who inspire me to be creative and to have fun! —G.L.T.

To my mother, Edmina Janus, who taught me to cook and to love to cook.

—K.J.K.

Text copyright © 2015 by Sylvia Rouss
Illustrations copyright © 2015 by Kathrine Janus Kahn

All rights reserved. International copyright secured. No part of this book may be reproduced, stored in a retrieval system, or transmitted in any form or by any means—electronic, mechanical, photocopying, recording, or otherwise—without the prior written permission of Lerner Publishing Group, Inc., except for the inclusion of brief quotations in an acknowledged review.

KAR-BEN PUBLISHING
A division of Lerner Publishing Group, Inc.
241 First Avenue North
Minneapolis, MN 55401 USA
1-800-4-Karben

Website address: www.karben.com

Main body text set in Times Europa Roman.
Typeface provided by Adobe Systems.

Library of Congress Cataloging-in-Publication Data

Rouss, Sylvia A.
    Sammy Spider's first taste of Hanukkah : a cookbook / by Sylvia A. Rouss and Genene Turndorf ; illustrated by Katherine Janus Kahn.
        pages   cm.
    ISBN: 978–1–4677–5237–4 (lib. bdg. : alk. paper)
    1. Hanukkah cooking—Juvenile literature. 2. Hanukkah—Juvenile literature.
    I. Turndorf, Genene, author. II. Kahn, Katherine, illustrator. III. Title. IV. Title: First taste of Hannukkah.
    TX739.2.H35R68 2015
    641.5'67435—dc23   2014028830

Manufactured in the United States of America
1 – VP – 7/15/15

j641.567435 Rou

3357769

Table of Contents

Introduction

Sammy Spider dangled from his web as Mr. Shapiro told Josh the story of the Maccabees and the miracle of the oil:

"A small group of Jews called the Maccabees defeated the Greeks who ruled over them. The Maccabees took back the Holy Temple and relit the Temple menorah with a tiny bit of oil that they thought would burn for one day. A miracle happened and it burned for eight days!"

"We celebrate Hanukkah by lighting the candles in the menorah," added Mrs. Shapiro. "We will light one more candle each night until all eight candles are burning brightly."

"Can we celebrate Hanukkah, too?" Sammy asked his mother.

"Silly little Sammy," Mrs. Spider laughed. "Spiders don't celebrate Hanukkah. Spiders spin webs! But you may watch the Hanukkah festivities while you spin."

Sammy was eager to watch the Shapiros cook delicious foods and make Hanukkah decorations. He listened as Mr. and Mrs. Shapiro told Josh the eight rules for cooking in the kitchen:

1. Wash your hands before and after touching food.
2. Keep your fingers out of your mouth.
3. Turn your head if you have to cough or sneeze.
4. Before you start making a recipe, gather all the ingredients and cooking utensils you will need.
5. Follow the directions as an adult reads the recipe.
6. Because knives are sharp, plastic knives are best for children.
7. Have an adult help with the use of an oven, stove, electrical appliance, or sharp utensils.
8. Have an adult handle hot dishes.

"I know how I can help," Sammy said with a smile. "I'm going to show Josh which recipes are Meat, Dairy, or Parev by spinning M, D, or P in our web!"

Meat　　　　　　Dairy　　　　　　Parev

Sammy Spider's Simple Snacks

Maccabee Munch

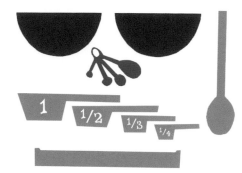

Sammy Spider says you will need:

2 large mixing bowls

1 mixing spoon

1 set of measuring cups

1 set of measuring spoons

13 x 9-inch baking pan

Ingredients:

2 cups toasted wheat cereal squares

2 cups toasted corn cereal squares

1 cup dried apples

¼ cup melted margarine

⅓ cup brown sugar

2 Tablespoons light corn syrup

1 teaspoon cinnamon

½ cup dried cranberries

½ cup raisins

½ cup yogurt-covered raisins

Directions:

1. Preheat the oven to 325°.

2. In one bowl, mix the wheat squares, corn squares and dried apples.

3. In another bowl, mix the melted margarine, brown sugar, light corn syrup, and cinnamon.

4. Add the wet mixture to the dry mixture. Stir until well blended.

5. Pour into a 13x9 baking pan.

6. Bake for 15 minutes.

7. Toss with dried cranberries, raisins, and yogurt-covered raisins and serve.

Yummy! I love fruit! Yummy! I love fruit!..

Fruity De-lights

Sammy Spider says you will need:

2 mixing bowls

1 set of measuring cups

1 set of measuring spoons

1 fork

Toothpicks

Ingredients:

¼ cup sour cream

1 Tablespoon brown sugar

¼ teaspoon cinnamon

¼ teaspoon vanilla

Variety of fruits (grapes, strawberries, pineapple chunks, apple slices)

Directions:

1. Wash the fruit and place in one bowl.

2. Use a fork to mix the sour cream, brown sugar, cinnamon, and vanilla in the other bowl.

3. Spear the fruit with a toothpick and dip into the sour cream mixture.

Yummy! I love fruit! Yummy! I love fruit!

Crispy Potato Veggies

Sammy Spider says you will need:

2 mixing bowls

1 set of measuring cups

1 set of measuring spoons

1 fork

1 mixing spoon

1 cookie sheet

Ingredients:

1 cup instant mashed potatoes (dry)

1 Tablespoon garlic powder

1 cup Parmesan cheese

4 Tablespoons melted butter or margarine

4 eggs

Variety of raw sliced vegetables (zucchini, broccoli, mushrooms, carrots, cauliflower)

Cooking spray

Directions:

1. Preheat the oven to 400°.
2. Use a spoon to mix the dry mashed potatoes, garlic powder, Parmesan cheese, and butter together in one bowl.
3. In another bowl, crack the eggs and beat them with a fork.
4. Dip the vegetables in the beaten eggs and then in the potato mixture.
5. Grease the cookie sheet with cooking spray.
6. Place the vegetables on the greased cookie sheet.
7. Bake for 10-12 minutes until crispy.

Candle-Glow Biscuits

Sammy Spider says you will need:

1 cheese grater

1 large mixing bowl

1 mixing spoon

1 set of measuring cups

1 set of measuring spoons

1 cookie sheet

Ingredients:

1 8-ounce block of cheddar cheese

3 cups flour

1¼ cups softened butter

2 teaspoons baking powder

1½ cups milk

Cooking spray

Directions:

1. Preheat the oven to 400°.
2. Shred the cheese with the grater until you have 4 cups of shredded cheese.
3. Mix the cheese, flour, butter and baking powder in large mixing bowl.
4. Slowly mix in the milk.
5. Spray the cookie sheet with cooking spray.
6. Drop spoonfuls of the batter onto the greased cookie sheet.
7. Bake for 10-12 minutes.

Applesauce by Josh!

Sammy Spider says you will need:

1 set of measuring cups

1 apple corer

1 plastic knife

1 paring knife

1 cooking pot with a lid

1 wooden spoon

1 potato masher

1 vegetable peeler

Ingredients:

3-4 large apples (4 cups when chopped)   ½ cup sugar

1 cup apple juice   Juice of 1 lemon (2-3 Tablespoons)

Directions:

1. Have an adult peel and core the apples.

2. Use a plastic knife to cut the apples into chunks. You should have about 4 cups total.

3. Place the apple chunks in a cooking pot.

4. Mix in the sugar using the wooden spoon.

5. Stir in the apple juice.

6. Squeeze in the lemon juice and mix.

7. Place a lid on the cooking pot and cook on a low-medium setting for 45 minutes until the apples are tender and chunky.

8. Remove the pot from the stove and let the applesauce cool.

9. Use a potato masher to make the applesauce as mushy as you want.

Mashing

WOW!

Sweet Potato Gelt

Sammy Spider says you will need:

1 large mixing bowl

1 medium mixing bowl

1 set of measuring cups

1 potato masher

1 can opener

1 gallon-sized plastic zipper bag

1 rolling pin

1 foil-lined cookie sheet

Ingredients:

1 16-ounce can of sweet potatoes

1 8-ounce can of pineapple

2 cups corn flakes

Directions:

1. Preheat the oven to 350°.

2. Use a can opener to open sweet potato and pineapple cans, and drain the juice.

3. Put the sweet potatoes into a large bowl and mash with the potato masher.

4. Add the pineapple, and mash some more.

5. Pour the corn flakes into the plastic bag and seal it.

6. Use the rolling pin to crush the cereal inside the bag.

7. Pour the cereal crumbs into a medium bowl.

8. Use your hands to shape the mixture into patties and then dip into the corn flake crumbs.

9. Place on a foil-lined cookie sheet.

10. Bake for 15-20 minutes.

...and smashing......What fun!!!!

Sammy Spider's Miracle Meals

12

Maccabee and Cheese

Sammy Spider says you will need:

1 set of measuring cups

1 set of measuring spoons

1 large spoon or ladle

1 large mixing bowl

9-inch square baking dish or casserole dish

Ingredients:

Cooking spray

8 ounces of cooked pasta (some stores carry Hanukkah pasta in dreidel or star shapes)

2 Tablespoons melted butter

1 cup sour cream

1½ cups small curd cottage cheese

½ teaspoon salt

1 8-ounce package shredded cheddar cheese

Directions:

1. Preheat the oven to 375°.

2. Use a spoon to mix melted butter, sour cream, cottage cheese and one cup of shredded cheese in a bowl.

3. Mix in the pasta.

4. Spray the baking dish with cooking spray.

5. Spoon the pasta mixture into greased baking dish.

6. Sprinkle the remaining cheese on top.

7. Bake for 30 minutes or until bubbly.

Pocketful of Miracles

Sammy Spider says you will need:

8 small bowls

8 small spoons

1 plastic knife

1 set of measuring cups

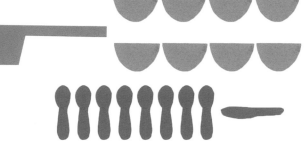

Ingredients:

Pita bread

½ pound cooked ground beef

2-3 tomatoes

1 can corn, drained

1-2 avocados

1 can olives

1 can black beans, rinsed and drained

1 head shredded lettuce

1-2 cups parev salad dressing or salsa

Directions:

1. Use a plastic knife to dice the tomatoes and avocado.

2. Place the tomatoes in one bowl and the avocado in a second bowl. Continue filling the remaining bowls with the other ingredients until all 8 bowls are filled.

3. Place a spoon in each bowl.

4. Cut the pita in half with the plastic knife.

5. Spoon the fillings into the pita, add dressing, and serve.

Little Latkes

Sammy Spider says you will need:

1 blender

1 mixing bowl

1 set of measuring cups

1 set of measuring spoons

1 frying pan

1 spatula

Ingredients:

3 cups cubed potatoes, unpeeled

1 quarter of an onion

3 Tablespoons flour

¼ cup milk

2 eggs

1 teaspoon salt

Oil for frying

Directions:

1. Put the onion, milk, flour, salt and eggs in a blender.

2. Add ½ cup of the potatoes.

3. Blend on medium speed for 5 seconds.

4. Add the remaining potatoes and blend for another 10 seconds, until the potatoes are grated.

5. Have an adult pour a small amount of oil in a frying pan and heat on medium-high setting.

6. Have an adult drop tablespoons full of latke batter into the frying pan to make small latkes.

7. Fry on both sides until crisp and brown.

15

Count-to-Eight Shishkebab

Sammy Spider says you will need:

1 metal skewer

1 cooking brush

1 small bowl

1 broiler pan

Ingredients:

2 pre-cooked turkey meatballs

2 cherry tomatoes

2 pineapple chunks

2 sweet peppers

¼ cup olive oil

Directions:

1. Carefully place 1 meatball, 1 cherry tomato, 1 pineapple chunk, and 1 sweet pepper on a skewer.

2. Add the other meatball, cherry tomato, pineapple chunk, and sweet pepper.

3. Count all the pieces of food on the skewer. There should be a total of 8!

4. Place the skewer on a broiler pan.

5. Pour the olive oil in a bowl.

6. Use a cooking brush to paint a little oil on the shishkebab.

7. Have an adult place the shishkebab under the broiler until food browns.

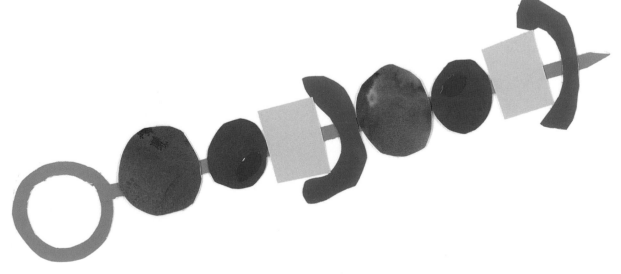

Pizza Spinners

Sammy Spider says you will need:

1 cookie sheet

1 set of measuring cups

1 set of measuring spoons

1 plastic knife

1 small bowl

Ingredients:

2 cans refrigerated crescent roll dough

4 Tablespoons Parmesan cheese

1 cup shredded Mozzarella cheese

1 12-oz. jar pizza sauce

Cooking spray

Directions:

1. Preheat oven to 350°.
2. Unroll refrigerated crescent roll dough and place on greased cookie sheet.
3. Combine the cheeses in a bowl.
4. Sprinkle cheese mixture on dough.
5. Roll and cut each piece into 6 slices using a plastic knife.
6. Bake for 13-15 minutes.
7. Place warm pizza sauce in a small bowl for dipping.

8-Cup Soup

Sammy Spider says you will need:

1 large soup pot

1 set of measuring cups

1 ladle

1 stirring spoon

Ingredients:

8 cups water

2 cubes vegetable bouillon

½ cup corn (fresh or frozen)

½ cup peas (fresh or frozen)

½ cup green beans (fresh or frozen)

1 cup diced carrots (fresh or frozen)

2 cups dry pasta

Salt and pepper

Directions:

1. Pour the water and vegetable bouillon into a pot.
2. Have an adult boil the soup on the stove.
3. Add the vegetables and pasta to the pot.
4. Let the soup simmer for 30 minutes, stirring often.
5. Add salt and pepper to taste.

Sammy Spider's Tasty Treats

Blue Shamash Shake

Sammy Spider says you will need:

1 blender

1 set of measuring cups

Drinking straws

Ingredients:

1 cup fresh or frozen blueberries

1 cup milk

1 cup blueberry yogurt

½ cup ice cubes (if using fresh berries)

Directions:

1. Put the blueberries in the blender.
2. Add the milk, yogurt, and ice cubes.
3. Blend until smooth.
4. Pour into the drinking cups.
5. Add the straws and start sipping!

Hanukkah Web Cake

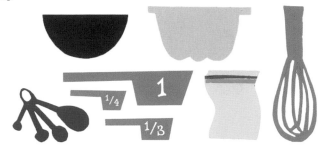

Sammy Spider says you will need:

1 large mixing bowl

1 whisk

1 Bundt pan

1 set of measuring cups

1 set of measuring spoons

1 small plastic baggie

Ingredients for Cake:

1 package butter cake mix

1 cup sour cream

⅓ cup oil

4 eggs

¼ cup water

¼ cup white sugar

1 Tablespoon flour

Cooking spray

Ingredients for Spider Web Icing:

2 cups powdered sugar

2 Tablespoons milk

Blue food coloring

Directions:

1. Preheat the oven to 375°.

2. Use the whisk to mix the sour cream, oil, eggs, water, sugar, and cake mix in a bowl.

3. Spray the Bundt pan with cooking spray, then coat with flour.

4. Pour the batter into Bundt pan and bake for 45-55 minutes.

5. Cool in the pan for 25 minutes before removing to a serving plate.

6. Mix the powdered sugar, milk, and 1 drop of blue food coloring in a small plastic baggie to make a glaze.

7. Poke a hole in one corner of the baggie and drizzle over the cake to create a Hanukkah spider web.

Melt-in-Your-Mouth Menorahs

Sammy Spider says you will need:
1 dinner plate
2 small bowls

Ingredients:
1 banana
9 marshmallows
9 pretzel sticks
Multicolored sprinkles

Directions:

1. Peel the banana and place on the plate.
2. Attach a mini-marshmallow to the end of a pretzel stick.
3. Repeat with the other marshmallows and pretzels.
4. Stick the free ends of the pretzels into the banana in a straight line.
5. Decorate with sprinkles.

Chocolate "Fun-due"

Sammy Spider says you will need:

1 microwave-safe bowl

1 set of measuring cups

1 large spoon

1 fork per person

Ingredients:

1 cup semisweet chocolate chips

½ cup half-and-half

1 banana, sliced

½ cup strawberries, sliced

½ cup marshmallows

½ cup pound cake cubes

½ cup pineapple chunks

½ cup apple slices

½ cup pear slices

½ cup peach slices

Directions:

1. Place the chocolate chips in bowl.

2. Pour in the half-and-half and mix with spoon.

3. Place in the microwave and heat for 45 seconds until the chocolate is melted and smooth.

4. Stir mixture with a spoon.

5. Use the fork to dip individual foods into chocolate and eat!

23

Delicious Dreidels

Sammy Spider says you will need:

1 plastic knife

1 plate

Ingredients:

8 chocolate candy kisses

8 large marshmallows

8 pretzel sticks

1 container vanilla frosting

Directions:

1. Spread a little vanilla frosting on the top of one marshmallow.

2. Spread a little vanilla frosting on the flat side of the chocolate kiss.

3. Attach the marshmallow to the chocolate kiss.

4. Push a pretzel stick through the marshmallow and into the chocolate kiss.

5. Repeat to make more.

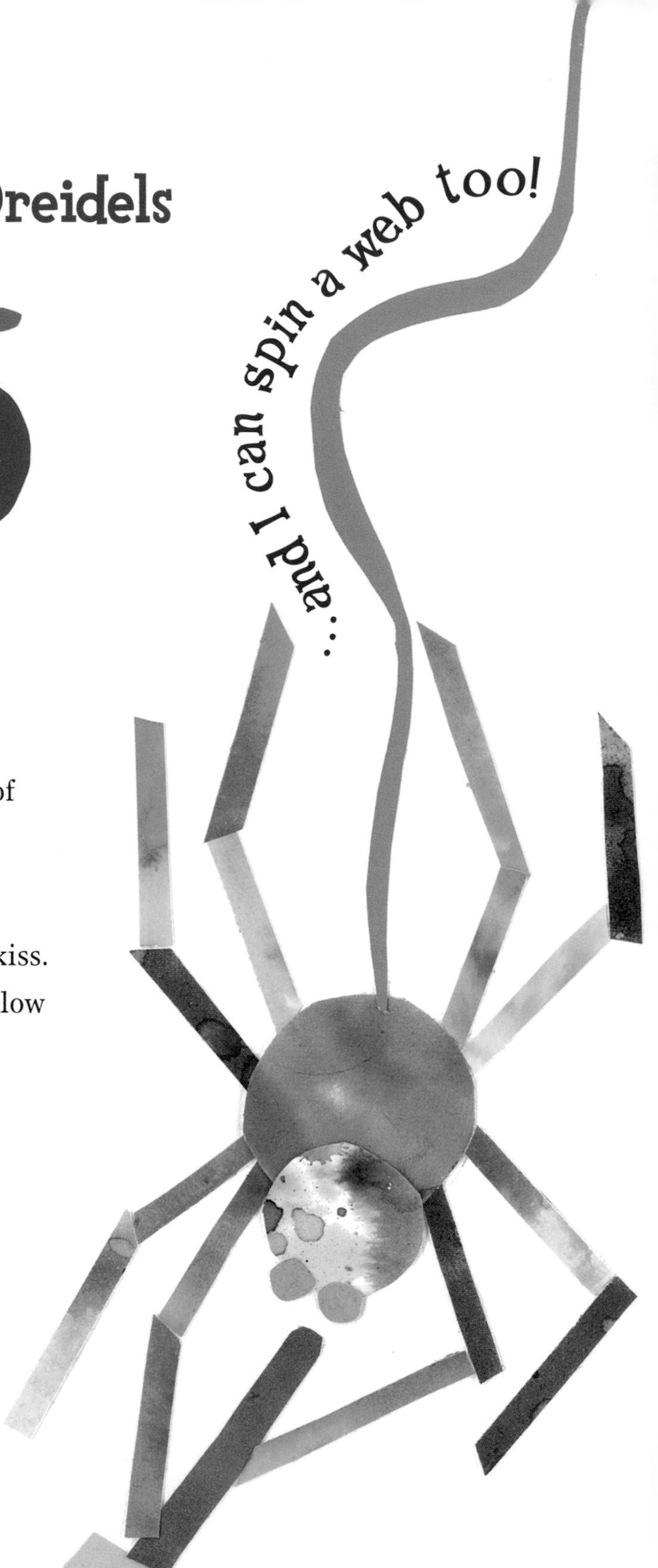

...and I can spin a web too!

I can spin the dreidel...

Gr8t-Tasting Smoothie

Sammy Spider says you will need:

1 blender

1 set of measuring cups

Drinking straws

Ingredients:

1 banana

1 cup strawberries (fresh or frozen)

1 cup mango (fresh or frozen)

1 cup apple juice

2 cups ice (if using fresh fruit)

Directions:

1. Combine strawberries, banana and mango in the blender.

2. Blend until fruit is pureed.

3. Add the juice (and ice if using fresh fruit) and blend until the mixture is thick and smooth.

4. Pour into the drinking cups.

5. Add the straws and start sipping!

Sammy Spider's Crafty Ideas

Menorah Magic

Sammy Spider says you will need:

1 piece of wood (2 inches wide by 2 feet long)

Blue and silver acrylic paint (optional)

1 paintbrush

8 small empty jars (such as baby food jars or jam jars)

1 larger empty jar

9 different types of candy

9 bolts

1 bottle of glue

Directions:

1. Paint the wood, and allow it to dry.
2. Wash, dry, and remove the labels from the jars.
3. Fill each jar with a different kind of candy.
4. Close each jar.
5. Using glue, attach the jars to the wood piece.
6. Place the larger jar in the middle for the Shammash.
7. Glue a bolt to the top of each jar to hold the candles.
8. On each night of Hanukkah, enjoy the candy from that jar.

Menorah Drip Mat

Sammy Spider says you will need:

8x11 poster board

Scraps of Hanukkah wrapping paper

Scissors and glue

Blue, silver, and gold glitter glue

Clear contact paper

Directions:

1. Cut the Hanukkah wrapping paper into 1- to 2-inch pieces.
2. Glue to the poster board.
3. Drizzle glitter glue over the poster board. Let dry.
4. Cover with the clear contact paper.
5. Place your family's menorah on top of the mat to catch the dripping candle wax.

Hanukkah Gift Wrap

Sammy Spider says you will need:

Old newspapers

Tempera paint in your favorite colors

Large sheets of white tissue paper

Paper plates

Hanukkah
 cookie cutters

Paper towels

Directions:

1. Cover your work area with newspaper.
2. Pour the paint colors onto the paper plates.
3. Place a sheet of tissue paper on top of the newspaper.
4. Dip a cookie cutter into the paint.
5. Blot the cookie cutter on a paper towel to remove extra paint.
6. Stamp the cookie cutter onto the tissue paper.
7. Repeat with as many cookie cutters as you like, as many times as you want.
8. Let dry and use to wrap gifts.

True Blue Play Dough

Sammy Spider says you will need:

1 set of measuring cups

1 set of measuring spoons

1 large mixing bowl

1 small pot

1 mixing spoon

1 airtight plastic container

2 cups flour

½ cup salt

4 teaspoons cream of tartar

2 Tablespoons baby oil

2 cups boiling water

Blue food coloring

Directions:

1. Combine the flour, salt, and cream of tartar in a bowl.
2. Add the boiling water, oil, and food coloring.
3. Mix well with a spoon and let the mixture cool.
4. Take the mixture out of the bowl and knead it. Add a bit more flour if the dough feels too sticky.
5. Store in an airtight plastic container.

Salt Dough Hanukkah Decorations

Sammy Spider says you will need:

1 set of measuring cups

1 large mixing bowl

1 mixing spoon

1 rolling pin

Hanukkah cookie cutters

1 toothpick

1 foil-lined cookie sheet

Blue, gold, and silver acrylic paints

3 paintbrushes

Ribbon

Ingredients:

1 cup salt

2 cups flour

1 cup water

Directions:

1. Use the spoon to mix the flour and salt in the mixing bowl.

2. Mix in the water a little at a time.

3. Knead the dough for 5 minutes. Add a bit more flour if the dough feels too sticky.

4. Roll out the dough to ¼-inch thickness.

5. Use the Hanukkah cookie cutters to cut shapes.

6. Poke a hole at the top of your shapes with a toothpick.

7. Place on a cookie sheet.

8. Bake at 325° for 30 minutes or let shapes air dry over several days.

9. Decorate with the paints.

10. String a ribbon through the hole at the top for hanging.
    (Optional: glue a magnet to the back of the decoration to create a refrigerator magnet.)

Sammy Spider Spinning Puppet

Sammy Spider says you will need:

1 large paper plate

1 small paper plate

Scissors

1 sheet blue construction paper

1 sheet yellow construction paper

Glue

2 large "wiggle eyes"

8 dreidel stickers

Crayons

Directions:

1. Color the paper plates in your favorite colors.

2. Glue the plates together to create Sammy Spider's body and head.

3. Glue two "wiggly eyes" to the small paper plate.

4. Cut four 1-inch strips from yellow construction paper.

5. Cut four 1-inch strips from blue construction paper.

6. Glue the eight strips onto Sammy's body.

7. Fold each strip up in the middle to look like a spider leg.

8. Place a dreidel sticker on each of Sammy's feet.

9. Glue the craft stick to the bottom of Sammy's body and let dry.

10. Hold the stick between two hands and rub together to make Sammy twirl and spin his dreidels.

Lighting the Menorah

The shammash, the helper candle, is always the first candle lit on the menorah. On the first night of Hanukkah the shammash is used to light the first candle, which is placed on the right side of the menorah. Each night one more candle is added.

The Hanukkah Blessings

Baruch Atah Adonai Eloheinu Melech Ha'olam asher kid'shanu b'mitzvotav v'tzivanu l'hadlik ner shel Hanukkah.

Blessed are You, Lord our God, King of the universe, who has sanctified us with Your commandments, and commanded us to kindle the Hanukkah light.

Baruch Atah Adonai Eloheinu Melech Ha'olam she'asah nisim la'avoteinu bayamim hahem baz'man hazeh.

Blessed are You, Lord our God, King of the universe, who performed miracles for our forefathers in those days, and at this time.

On the first night of Hanukkah, this blessing is added:

Baruch Atah Adonai Eloheinu Melech Ha'olam shehechiyanu v'kiy'manu v'higianu lazman hazeh.

Blessed are You, Lord our God, King of the universe, who has granted us life, sustained us, and enabled us to reach this occasion.

Sylvia A. Rouss is an award-winning author and early childhood educator, and the creator of the popular Sammy Spider series which recently celebrated its 20th anniversary with over half a million Sammy Spider books sold. She lives in Tarzana, California.

Genene Levy Turndorf is a graduate of Stephens College with a degree in Early Childhood and Elementary Education. She is an educator at a Jewish preschool in Los Angeles. Combining her love of creating and exploring with young children with her love of cooking, she has developed a popular cooking class for young children. This is her first children's book.

Katherine Janus Kahn has illustrated more than 50 picture books, toddler board books, holiday services, and activity books. She and her Sammy Spider puppet visit schools and bookstores for felt board storytelling. She lives in Silver Spring, Maryland.